There's A Stranger In My House

"The Silent Screams Series"
Part III

Book Design by: Ronika Hughes with
Ambri'ance Graphic Design
ambriancedesign@gmail.com

There's A Stranger In My House

Author: Yolanda Lee~George

While the publisher has made every attempt to release correct addresses and contact information at the time of this publication, the publisher assumes no responsibility for errors or changes that come about after the publish date.

All rights reserved. No part of this book may be reproduced, scanned, or distributed in any printed or electronic forms existing now or in the future without written permission from the publisher. For information regarding permission, please write to:

Black~Butterfly Publishing
www.bethanysgroup.com
Yolanda@bethanysgroup.com

Please help in the fight against piracy of Copyrighted materials. Purchase only authorized editions.

ISBN-13: 978-0-9910760-2-4 © 2014
Black~Butterfly Publishing Inc.
ISBN-10: 0991076028
All rights reserved. Published 2014.
Printed in the United States of America.

Autograph Page

Acknowledgments

I have to acknowledge the Lord Jesus Christ who is certainly the head of my life, who's taken me through dangers seen and unseen, who's protected me and my family even in the midst of the storms. I'm nothing without you Lord, I can't do anything without you Lord, but I can do ALL things, through Christ that strengthens me.

To my children (oldest to youngest) **Nijah Lee, Johnna Lee, Johntavia Wallace, Johnavia Wallace** and **John Wallace III**; thank a million times over for allowing me to continually air our dirty past so that others may be healed by our story, to allow others to know that they are not alone just because they are in church (things happen in the church also). I can't thank you all enough for being my strong towers through all of this and I want you to know that I love you dearly. I have to acknowledge my grandbabies because one day, this same book may have to help them, help someone else, so thank you in advance, Nijon Lee, Nija'e Lee, Na'Zariyah Lee and Heaven Wallace~Edmond, and my 2 unborn grand's Ni'Aisa Lee and still waiting on the sex of the other from my son John Wallace, III ☺ I love you all!

Most of all I have to thank my husband **Lorenzo George, Sr.** for knowing my past, my hurts and all that came with me, for loving me through airing my dirty past and still loving me through it, even when I wasn't sure which way to go Thank you baby, I Love You!

I must give a separate acknowledgement for Johntavia, for standing up and not being ashamed to tell your story, even when the enemy tried to tell the story the wrong way, even when the enemy tried to shame you, you still got up on your feet and realized, there's more Johntavia's out there like you that needed to hear your story. I'm proud of you and I know that although this may have been detrimental to your flesh, God is going to use this to take you to another level; this is your testimony baby, so stand up and shout unto the Lord with gladness because it could've been just a little bit worst. Some people died, some people were penetrated, some people committed suicide and the list goes on and on. I know it may seem like WHY ME, but Mother Gooden use to say "Why NOT YOU"…allow God to get the glory out of this…it's just begun! I love you!

Last but NEVER least but always the best: Raymond J. Lee, Sr., my daddy, my heartbeat, my strength, my everything next to God. From a child you told me I could do all things, you told me to pray without ceasing, you told me not to let the enemy see me sweat, and you've always told me you were proud of me. Daddy you're part of the reason I can keep going hard! I love you so very much!

Special Thanks

Special thanks to **Leon & Sabrina Chandler**, for ALWAYS encouraging me to go forward and seeing in me what I don't see in myself.

Felecia "Cookie" Lee for having faith in me through everything I do and being that ear that's always open to hear me, encourage me and aggravate. ☺

Pastor Prophetess Brown thank you for allowing God to speak through you into my life; I thank God for everything I learned while under your leadership; thank you for continually reminding me of Isaiah 54:17 NO WEAPON, I love you dearly.

Pastor McKinney for speaking life into me for such a long time, for praying for me and covering me and I didn't even know it. I thank God for the divine connection that HE has allowed us to have. I thank God that although my Spiritual Mommy (Eddie Mae Gooden) is gone home with the Lord…God already had you standing in the shadows with open arms to receive me, I'm grateful to God for being under such an awesome leadership and such a powerful anointing. I thank God that I was chosen to be your Spiritual Daughter!

To all that see more in me than I see in myself, I appreciate you and love you very much. If I missed anyone, charge it to my brain and not my heart!

RONIKA HUGHES I LOVE YOU GIRL!

Table of Contents

Chapter 1 – Finally I'm free (or was I)?

Chapter 2 – Serving the people instead of God!

"PAUSE"

Chapter 3 – Here come the DEVIL!

Chapter 4 – Keep your eyes on the kids!
"Ugly Spirits Within!"

Chapter 5 – There's a Stranger in my house
"What is my radar picking up?"

Chapter 6 – MOMA DON'T KILL HIM!
"The Prayers of the Righteous"

Chapter 7 – Obeying the voice of God!

Chapter 8 – Where do we go from here?

Chapter 9 – Lord I see more demons ahead!

Chapter 10 – Picking up the pieces and moving on!

Rap by: Ronika Hughes

Excerpt from Tae's story!

Introduction

Some of you have read Parts I and II of my III Part series **"The Silent Scream Series"**, in **Part *I* "Someone to Love the Little Girl in Me"** you read about a woman that grew up being verbally, mentally and emotionally abused, a woman that was so broken and so needing to be validated, a woman with low self-esteem, a woman that danced, stripped, sold drugs, used drugs and was very promiscuous and looking for love in all the wrong places, trying to fill a void that only God could fill and she didn't even know it. A woman that had to portray a hard-core image to get by and her defense mechanisms were to be mean, hard and not care about the world around her, a woman that hid behind the **silent screams** in her life. Her **silent screams** were her screams within her own self, looking for a light at the end of the tunnel that wasn't even there. Afraid of her own self, afraid to confront her own issues and pretended everything in her life was just great. When some late nights alone, she cried herself to sleep and no-one even knew but God.

In **Part II "Someone Almost Loved Me to Death"** you read about a woman that wanted to be loved so badly, she met someone that almost loved her to death for 10 ½ yrs. while her children by stood helplessly and watched. She stayed because she wanted to be loved at first, but then the love became fear and she had nowhere else to turn to. This man told her he loved her till death, that he would kill for her and even kill her if he had to if she ever tried to leave him. What she didn't know was, this guy was looking for something just as she was, and he too had **Silent Screams** of his own.

She quickly learned the true meaning of the saying **"where there is Good, Evil is always present"** *Romans 7:19-21* and "the devil won't come to you in a red suit and a pitch fork, he will come with all the nice things to say, dressed in a suit" and so he did.

Now here we are in Part III **"There's A Stranger In My House"**, *SOME NAMES HAVE BEEN CHANGED FOR LEGAL PURPOSES AND PROTECTION.*

Yolanda and her 5 children went forward with the mindset that they needed to begin to heal, it wasn't always easy though. She was still very vulnerable emotionally, her mind was still a bit twisted mentally and everything was still so out of whack for her because she'd been controlled for so long, now she was rearranging herself again because now she was a single mother raising her now broken children, working full-time and trying to keep the family in church.

She was in church 6 days a week (thinking that was healthy), but lost focus of reality. She was in church for the wrong reasons (not that she wasn't serving God) but she was there so much, she began to serve the PEOPLE, and it wasn't always God that she was worshipping or trying to satisfy, it was the people that was watching her that she was satisfying 85% of the time – if not more. She was in church because **THE PEOPLE** said she needed to be in church every time the doors open, she needed to do this, that and the other, to a point she actually wasn't there for the business of the Lord, she was there for the pleasing of the people. She didn't realize she was still trying to be wanted and fit in (she replaced one bad habit with another) **PEOPLE PLEASE BE CAREFUL THAT YOU'RE SERVING GOD AND NOT THE PEOPLE.** Getting so wrapped up in the things of the **CHURCH** Yolanda didn't pay attention to the devil in the sheep's clothing **Matthew 7:15** (*we'll just call him M.T.*) sitting right there in the church watching her worship.

Part III takes you into a world of how important it is to HEAL HEAL HEAL before moving forward in certain things. Hear the voice of GOD and don't move until you've gotten past your hurt, anger, fear, revenge and whatever else is undone; your spiritual sensors will be off and you'll find yourself in a new kind of mess! My focus was off and I allowed A Stranger in My House; that came out of the church. This stranger came in a violated my child, with his smooth talk and cunning ways. People of God, DO NOT be deceived by the tricks of the enemy, gird yourself up and put on the whole armor of God and hear what the Spirit of the Lord is saying to the church/US!

Chapter 1 – Finally I'm Free (or was I)!

After I got my divorce and my ex-husband was in prison for 6 yrs. for all the charges against me, I felt free and was able to breath and not look over my shoulder all the time. Although I was free from the physical, I still had my good and bad days emotionally and mentally. I was going to church with my kids and was looking forward to a better life. Being in church felt like my security blanket, but I was in church around the clock, Tuesday choir rehearsal, Wednesday bible study, Thursday kids choir rehearsal, Friday the church was always having an event "Friday Family Fun Night" and we had to be there, Saturday early morning prayer at 6am and I stayed there for hours after prayer, Sunday I was there for early morning prayer, regular service and then came back evening service at 6pm (with my kids). I was dedicated to the things of the Lord at first, but then I became dedicated to the **CHURCH**. I enjoyed being there with the Spiritual Mothers and being able to sing in the choir, hang with the ladies and fellowship with a smile (the smile was becoming a pretense because I was slowly putting myself in a church bondage), having no one to control when I was allowed to talk, bathe, eat, sleep etc. I was completely ignoring the cry of my children although they enjoyed being at church sometimes too, I begin to replace the church for my ex-husband and my children needed me. Although it appeared I was free and I could spend more quality time with my children, I actually didn't. Listening to everyone tell me to be in church around the clock and that would be good for me and my children (don't get me wrong, being in church did have it's extremely great points for me and the kids, but I needed to have a balance and I didn't) I was at my spiritual mother's house everyday (with my kids) and it was bible study, church, and more church. My kids were having fun being able to actually not run and hide, sleep in the parks, church etc., but we weren't home a lot due to being at the church. We felt free, no more bondage in our lives (so I thought) and we didn't have to sleep in the car anymore. We enjoyed living in our beautiful home out in Valrico, FL, it was a brand new house and the kids loved it, they went to the local schools in the area and begin their little lives.

The kids and I were going to different functions at the church, we didn't have to rush home and it was good. I was doing a lot of fasting and praying, I worked the altar, sung in the choir and just helped anywhere that I could (not realizing I was still filling a void the wrong way). I was one of the prayer warriors in the church as well.

There was this one particular guy that had been around me and the kids for a long time because he was the head deacon in the church M.T. (a pillar as some called him) he would still pray with me, we'd talk all the time and he also taught children's church. My kids didn't like him in church that much and neither did a lot of the other kids but he was very stern and I felt he wanted the kids to learn so that's why the kids didn't like him (they didn't like structure). He lived with my spiritual mother because he and his wife were going through some changes. Him and I studied quite a bit when I was to my spiritual mother house, but I do recall her telling me to stay away from him because he liked me, but of course I didn't pay that any attention because I surely didn't like him that way so it really didn't matter. So I continued on with our bible study but I noticed my mommy still was very watchful. He would always compliment me (as he did when I was going through the abuse) and he would tell me to keep my head held high because I was beautiful and that made me smile (mind you I had a broken front tooth at that time).

Chapter 2 ~ Serving the people instead of God

1 Corinthians 7:22-24 NJKV
For he who is called in the Lord while a slave is the Lord's freedman. Likewise he who is called while free is Christ's slave. You were bought at a price; do not become slaves of men. Brethren, let each one remain with God in that state in which he was called!

I was starting to be pulled in every direction by people of the church and I started to feel controlled again, not paying it any attention, I was still not able to say NO and stand on it, I was still acting like a child to the people in the church, I didn't want to lose the love that I was getting from them. I started realizing that I wasn't paying my kids any attention, their homework was being left undone or half done because they couldn't get me to be still out of the church long enough to deal with my household (I was still filling a void).

I urge you to have a relationship with God in your heart first, and then have a relationship with the people of God. Yes I realize that it's important to fellowship, but be careful not to begin serving the people of God and not serving God! I say that realizing that God called us to fellowship one with another and it's important to do that. When you start to attend services that you didn't want to attend, or take out private time from your children and with God because the PEOPLE asked you to do something; there's a problem... It's ok to spend time alone with God, you SHOULD and SUPPOSE to have special time set apart for just you and God, times that you need to be alone with God because something else is going on within, it's ok to tell someone that you have a meeting with God and not deviate from it or feel bad about it.

I was still so stuck on not wanting to be rejected I still said yes to everything. I can't blame the people; I have to blame myself because a nice and simple "NO I apologize but I already have something on my agenda", was all I had to say. Even if their response was negative, you still hold on to what you and God have going on.

There was a few times I said no and I felt that rejection and it really hurt me, so instead of voicing my feelings I eventually left the church completely. (Please understand...don't let anyone fool you into believing that just because you're asked to do something in the church you HAVE to do it or you're a bad person, you're out of the will of God blah blah blah, especially if you already have plans, that means that person may need to check themselves for trying to make you feel guilty SHAME ON THEM, now please know, if it's something you can do, please do it with Love but if you're doing it because you don't want the Pastor or the members to be upset than you're doing it for the wrong reason, that's what made me leave the church, feeling guilty and not knowing how to say NO and doing it for the PEOPLE and not God. Do it from the heart and God will honor it (that's just my personal view, everyone's view is different). Yet again leaving the church was one of the biggest mistakes in the world (**PLEASE DO NOT LEAVE YOUR CHURCH IF GOD DIDN'T GIVE YOU PERMISSION TO LEAVE IT – DO NOT DO IT!**).

After leaving the church I had time to be with my kids and it felt good and they were happy, but then there was many of days (especially Saturday mornings when I'm normally in early morning prayer service) Sundays (when I'm there to pray through the church with the Saints of God), I was missing my worship. Although I worshipped at home, I prayed with my kids and I continued to fast, I felt emptiness inside of me. I begin to try and visit other churches, still missing the apostolic atmosphere and my leadership; it was almost a feeling of being lost. I tried to make the best of it. I wouldn't answer the phone for any of the saints, my church mothers or any one. I didn't know what to say, I felt butterflies in my stomach and a feeling of fear and that was because I replaced the people in the church for my ex-husband and I was pleasing the people of the church and not pleasing myself, my children or God (completely).

"PAUSE"

LET'S PAUSE HERE FOR A MOMENT AND GET SOME INFORMATION ON M.T.

The devil was teaching bible study, the pillar in the church and the head deacon (you have to remember that Satan worked very close to God and he was cunning). We need to learn (**Eph. 4:13~14**) *Till we all come in the unity of the faith, and the knowledge of the Son of God, unto the perfect man, unto the measure of the stature of the fullness of Christ: That we henceforth be no more children, tossed to and fro, and carried about with every wind of doctrine, by the sleight of men, and cunning craftiness, whereby they lie in wait to deceive;* It wasn't that Yolanda was tossed to and fro and carried about by every wind of doctrine, She was vulnerable and not watchful; Satan came in when he saw her weakness and she trusted him. She only moved to another form of hurt and still felt she needed to be validated and didn't realize it. She love hearing the word of God and love to hear someone bring forth the word of God in truth. Don't get it twisted, this guy wasn't bringing false doctrine, he was bringing truth because he knew truth, he just used the word to manipulate the women and children. M.T. was cunning, he knew that bible inside and out, he could teach a bible study or go into the word much deeper than most Pastors could. M.T. sat back and learned Yolanda, learned her children and he knew her long before her divorce, he knew her when she was running and hiding, he was actually one of the members that stayed awake praying for her and the kids while she was on the run from her abusive ex-husband.

Some noticed that Yolanda was being watched by M.T. in a different way than Yolanda was even thinking; they all tried to warn her to stay clear of him because he was watching her in lust. Yolanda still being naïve and thinking that the people where just old fashion and didn't want anyone around her because she was one of their sacred ones, she was very anointed, she's a worshipper, but most of all she was still so fresh from being hurt and beat down physically, mentally and emotionally and they just wanted her to allow God to complete her healing. Yet she continued to converse with M.T., she was dancing with the cunning devil and didn't even realize it.

Nevertheless while dancing with the devil (even after warnings from her Spiritual Mother to stay away without reason) Yolanda was so vulnerable that she still needed someone to love the little girl in her. She allowed that devil to watch her and learn her (as she did with the first devil) but this time he used the word of God (and he knew it well) and he deceived her with the word. Yolanda disregarded the fact that he was going through a divorce (of course telling her all the bad parts about his soon to be ex-wife and not paying attention that there's two sides to every story…she was soon to find out). She didn't pay attention that the children in the church really didn't like M.T., she thought because he was so firm and serious about the word of God and he taught children's Sunday School, Yolanda just figured the kids didn't like him because they wanted to play in church but he didn't allow it.

So many of the women in the church were crazy about him and found him to be very attractive yet cunning. He was about 6'1, 250 pounds of solid weight, dark skinned and a truck driver, but the word of God rolled off the man tongue like you wouldn't believe, he could prophesy a word and it would come to pass. M.T. had a unique and rare anointing on him, one that he could lay hands on a sickness and draw the sickness out of your body onto his own (God had really anointed this man). So now why would anyone think anything was wrong! Even the Pastor's loved him as the pillar of the church! One of the Pastors said "When MT is good he's show nuff good, but we he's bad, he's horrifically bad".

Yolanda felt that she had gotten her security with a man of God but as a friend or brother. After all, she didn't go looking for him; she wasn't even looking at him in that way, although he was attractive, she saw him as a brother in the church. Her self-esteem was still very low, she still had a missing tooth in her mouth and on top of all that, he was right there in the church, she didn't come on to him, and he knew all of her hurts and pains and didn't care. M. T. always prayed over her, spoke life into her and ushered her into the presents of the Lord, because that's what he did and that's who he was, it was just in his character. "Who'd have thought that he was Satan in the flesh?"

Now as you prepare to finish reading onto the next Chapters...step back into the world of Yolanda again and read about a woman that had been hurt so much, she just wanted to stay at the feet of God and raise her children, she just wanted to be around the people of God and learn more about God. She wanted to step into the realm of her calling (whatever that may have been), share her testimony and help other people, while helping herself and her children.

Yolanda wanted to be in church around other Christian women, she'd been introduced to the life of being an Apostolic Pentecostal (after being raised Methodist and Baptist) she enjoyed being a part of the U.P.C. she loved the worship, she loved the word, and she loved speaking in tongues and singing in tongues because that was her personal time with the Lord.

First I'd urge you to be careful when coming out of a hurtful relationship; you are very vulnerable and can easily be taken advantage of. You tend to want or desire something or someone that will understand your hurt or be there to just help rub your hurt away... never thinking that you would get involved with that someone/something (rather it be with a man, woman, drugs, alcohol etc.) you just need that something or someone to be there to help you through these hard times, to help you through the hurtful nights you now face, all the alone time you'll now have; never realizing it, but you are now filling another void, you're replacing one thing for another, but that's not always the best help. Trust me, we all say "I'll never fall for (whatever the thing/person was that hurt you) again, now I know better REALLY"?

M.T. knew her pain personally (because she shared it with him), he's prayed with her, prayed and fast for her and has been a pillar for her so many times during her trials. He had been there so many times as she began her walk with the Lord. Due to the fact she was so vulnerable; she didn't even realize the man in the suit had a pitch fork hidden behind his back. Although she was raised in the church, she had no true understanding of the church, because she saw many so-called saints that went to church every time the doors opened but they still did bad things in and out of the church.

Nevertheless she wanted more of God and wanted her children to have more of God. What she didn't realize right away was the church is still made up of PEOPLE and people hurt people because they are human, just because they are in the church doesn't mean that they are pure and Holy, just because they are in the church every time the doors open doesn't mean they are what you see. Remember "where good is, evil is AWAYS present!

MOVING RIGHT ALONE WITH CHAPTER 3

Chapter 3~Here come the DEVIL!

I was still visiting different churches, still trying to fill/replace another void, never once standing still to take a breath longer than a few minute and allowing God to deal with me and only me; to fully hear what "Thus said the Lord for me". People from the church continued to try and contact me but again I was a shamed and didn't want to go back into the life of not knowing how to say NO.

Eventually M. T. contacted me, wanting to know how I was doing and what was going on with me (I hadn't heard from him in a long time). I had even hid from my Spiritual Mother so I didn't know what was going on with M. T.

When he called me it was like a relief to hear from someone that I thought was real and wouldn't judge me for leaving the church, maybe he'd pray for me or give me a word of encouragement and that's exactly what he did. We talked on the phone for hours and M. T. finally told me he'd left the church as well because it was too much going on and all the blah blah of his stories (which I found out later was lies) and I told him about the kids and I visiting different church's and he was interested in going with us and so he did.

I allowed him to come to the house to change clothes because he'd said he was sleeping in his truck because his ex-wife had been going to our spiritual mother's house (mommy Gooden was both of our spiritual mother), so he'd take showers at the rest stop. He'd just came in from a route that morning (so he said) so he came over, took a shower and we all went to church and we enjoyed it. I cooked and we just sat and talked until it was time for him to get back to the truck and it was fun.

After he'd left, he called me as he prepared to go out on another route, but that wasn't unusual, he always called me out on his route and we'd talk on the phone while he was driving. He'd call me and we'd do bible study over the phone and when he get back in town I'd take him food if I'd cooked and go sit up at the truck stop and talk to him. After about a month or so he called and said that his air went out in his truck and he was going to rent a room for the weekend, so I offered him to use my son room and said that my son could come downstairs and sleep with me (he was about 3 or 4 yrs. old) and that's what he did. He said it would take a few days before the air was fixed.

Finally my Spiritual Mother called me again and I answered because I was hurting from not hearing her voice and I needed my mommy (I always need my MOMMY R.I.P mommy). When I answered she just cried and told me how much she missed me and asked what I'd been doing. I told her why I left and she shared some things with me that made me feel so much better but I also felt bad because had I spoken with her before I left the church, I would've still been there with my church family. I just needed to say NO and do what God said to do.

Then I told her about M.T. and I still being in contact with each other and what had transpired and she wasn't happy, she again told me to be careful and watch M.T. and that M.T. liked younger women/girls but I thought she meant younger like me being a few years younger than him, I didn't realize she was saying YOUNG LIKE IN CHILD AGE – EXACTLY!

I still ignored my Spiritual Mother because I'd been around M.T. so long and I didn't see the person she told me about in him and I thought my mommy just still wanted me to take it easy and not get involved with anyone, and I didn't have an attraction to M.T. not even in a sexual way. I just enjoyed being around him sharing the word with me and making me laugh. I've always been the type of woman that liked a man that was able to teach me something in the word of God or share in a word with me and he was a man filled with word (my biological daddy is a man of wisdom and word).

As time went on, M.T. was still to my house after a month saying that the truck still wasn't fixed. He then told me of his attraction to me and I still just smiled it off, and he continued to compliment me (of course my mouth was fixed by now).

It had been so long since a man told me I was pretty or any form of compliment because I stayed clear of men because I didn't want to be hurt – to me M.T. was exempt because I didn't like him in that way. Not knowing he was working his pitchfork into me by the everyday compliments, saying how I need a man of God that will keep me protected, usher me into the presents of the Lord, keep my crown covered as well as the kids etc. and that he was that man (and truthfully if he wasn't a DEVIL he could've been that man for someone).

The compliments continued and my flesh began to come weak and I started to receive the compliments in a different way than normal. M.T. had asked if he could come downstairs with me a few times and I laughed and played it off saying NO and I was glad my son and my youngest daughter was sleeping with me because I didn't want to give in.

Well one night while I was sleeping, I felt someone in my room touch my arm, it had to be about 2 a.m. and I woke up to see M.T. standing on the side of my bed. He asked me to move over so I did (I'm thinking something is bothering him and he's going to sit down on the side of the bed and talk to me about whatever it was) M.T. began to kiss me and I told him that wasn't a good idea, but he continued and I allowed my flesh to give in, I slept with M.T. and regretted it to the next morning…I regretted it because I wasn't married and being in the apostolic doctrine, I learned about sleeping around out of wedlock, the fornication and I felt nasty and I explained that to M.T., but of course he was cunning and manipulative, he broke it down to me and had me feeling like it wasn't that bad, God wasn't THAT angry with me because we were both saints (some blah blah blah mess), now in my heart of hearts I knew that it was bullcrap and that God wasn't pleased and I repented and tried to move forward.

Finally M.T. air got fixed in the truck but he'd still come by and do bible study with me, still go to church and just hang out over there on Sunday's for dinner. I didn't have another man in my life and wasn't looking for one. M.T. constantly asked me to be his wife and everything in me kept saying no but my mouth got afraid to say the word No again because he'd helped me through so many hard times I didn't want to lose my support system. I finally gave in with everything in my little naive mind saying **DO NOT DO IT**, we did the paperwork at the court house, I didn't want a wedding because I didn't want anyone to know that I was going to marry him, I wanted it to be a secret. After the 3 days went by, we went to the courthouse on my lunch break and I married him, so ashamed and embarrassed I really began to shut down emotionally inside but I didn't show it, I didn't know what it was making me feel that way but I repented in my own way. I told my God-sister Sabrina and she heard the unsurity in my voice and she questioned it but I continued on. I immediately had an uneasy spirit come over me (not realizing that uneasy spirit had just showed me that I'd married the devil). I knew then that the Holy Spirit was still with me, but I know that I was grieving the Holy Spirit within because of my ignorance and being naïve yet again!

I continued on and continued to pray. After a while I figured it wasn't that bad, for the most part he was gone during the week on the truck, he came in on the weekend, but we still hadn't found a church home. I was missing my life at my old church.

I'd told my Spiritual Mother about me marrying M.T. and it hurt her so bad, but because of her love for me she continued to pray for me and I guess she broke the news to the other leaders at the church. My Bishop was furious and that hurt me because I didn't understand why they didn't want me to be happy.

Finally I set up a meeting with my Bishop and we met, he talked to us, I asked for forgiveness for not coming to him and getting his blessings before I married M.T. and he was honest, he told me if I'd come to him he would have forbidden it and I was shocked, he said he had his reasons but being as we've gotten married, he'd keep us in prayer and would allow us back to the church (I didn't want to go back without his blessings and he still never gave it to us). I still felt uneasy so I found out that one of the other brothers of the church that had prophesied over my life so many of times, had been placed under Bishop as a Daughter Church in another area, so I went to visit and I felt so good to be back in the house of God with my family. Pastor Collins (who use to be brother Collins) welcomed us AFTER giving us a nice talk and voiced his opinion, he wanted us to utilize our gifts in the church, he welcomed us and honored what we'd done although he would not give his full true blessings either, being as he knew what others knew but no one would tell ME.

    I started my family back at church and it was good, but my attention was still all over the place, spirits running wild within me and I was unsure why. I was in position at the church, back on the battlefield of being a prayer warrior, setting the atmosphere for the Lord and helping usher people into the Holy Ghost and praying them through into deliverance, singing in the choir and just moving in every direction God had me to move in and it was good.

My children where back in Sunday school having fun with the youth and they were happy. M.T. was put back into Ushering (the church was small because it was a starter church). Yet there was something missing in my family, there was still yet an uneasy spirit and I was still tossing and turning within. I was still being wonder woman, working, taking care of the house, driving the kids back and forth to school, tending to my husband, positioning the church and just overwhelming myself as always.

Chapter 4 ~ Keep your eyes on the kids "Ugly Spirits Within!"

While being overwhelmed myself I allowed too much slack with my oldest daughter Taja, she started getting out more, M.T. would talk to her about life and men and being careful (not knowing when I wasn't around he was spitting venom into my baby spirit) while he was supposed to be talking to her for protection from the men and game in the streets, he was actually speaking sex into her and her little girl friends spirit and I didn't know this until later. My daughter came to me at the age of 15 and told me that M.T. told her he would take her to Victoria Secret and buy her some underclothes because it was time she started wearing big girl underwear, she didn't think it strange because he told her he was doing what a father would normally do for his daughter and she was excited because she didn't have a father figure that took the time to talk to her, we were too busy running and hiding from the abuse – although she did say she thought it was something I should be doing because she didn't know what to pick out with him. **IS there a stranger in my house?**

A red flag went up and I waited on him to get in from work, it was hard to hold my composure when asking him what in the hell did he mean by going to my child telling her he'd take her to a damn Victoria Secret, and he immediately went into defense mode because I was using curse words...something he'd never heard me use and he explained that he know that I be overwhelmed with daily stuff and he was asking if she needed anything and she said underclothes and he told her she was old enough to get cute panties for young ladies, he was going to speak to me about it and didn't mean any harm and he apologized, said that he was just trying to help me out and begin to allow them to see what having a father in their lives was all about. Although I was still uneasy I told him I appreciated what he was trying to do but he'd better never talk to my daughter about things such as that again and he assured me he wouldn't, that was the end of that and I pulled her and told her if he EVER spoke to her about private things like that again, she was to tell me immediately.

Time went on and my middle daughter Tae got sick and was too young to stay in the house alone, so he said he was doing a short run that day and she could go on the truck with him and he'd let her stay sleep in the cabin bed (now I know some may say geesh Yolanda all the red flags – but I honestly didn't see it from that angle, he'd been around us for about

10 yrs. in the church and I felt maybe some stuff I was just being to edgy about because of all that I'd been through). Nevertheless, I got off from work, they made it in from school/work and everything seemed fine. My daughter didn't seem to act any different, she didn't seem as if she was distant or anything, to me, she was still her little busy self.

Although my kids had started liking M.T. a long while back, for whatever reason, in due time they started to dislike M.T. again and when I'd question them why, they didn't comment and said they just didn't like him anymore. ***There's a Stranger in my house!!*** I told him how my children felt and he begins to say that they just want me to themselves because of all that we'd gone through and they had a jealousy because they were used to us being alone. So I just tried to give them more of my time to insure them that no one was coming in and taking our time away again.

Time continued to go on and the summer came, my middle daughter and son was in daycare because I had to work, my oldest daughter was doing summer school, my middle daughter had been acting out and crying when it was time to go to daycare and I didn't for the life of me understand why, she was maybe 11 or so and she'd always beg me not to send her to daycare and I'd ask her why and she'd just say she don't' want to take a nap but I told her that wasn't a good enough excuse because most of the time, the kids took naps at the daycares, and asked if there was something else going on and she kept saying no, I told her if something was wrong to please tell me because I'd take care of it (*I always told my kids if anyone touched them I'd kill them and didn't care if I had to spend the rest of my life in prison - BAD MISTAKE, I'LL EXPLAIN LATER*).

After summer was done and about a week later, my middle daughter use to always say to me "momma if I tell you something you won't' get mad with me will you" and I'd always say "no baby what is it" and she's say "never mind" and it would drive me insane because she did it every single time, so I yelled at her one day and said dammit if you're not going to tell me what's wrong stop asking me that and she cried, of course I apologized and we stayed quiet. Days went by and it pulled at me what she wanted to say so badly. I'm thinking it's something with M.T. and praying that it's not.

We had family meetings all the time and I constantly asked each of my children if they had a concern, if anything was bothering them, if anyone was bothering them etc. and the answer was always "No Ma"!

One morning I was about to get on the interstate and she said to me "mom if I tell you something will you get mad at me" I said again "No Tae, what is it, I won't get mad" but I was preparing myself to just ignore it because it had become a pattern of her saying never mind. I was driving full speed to merge onto the interstate when she said a family member had touched her, it was only by the grace of God that I didn't flip my car over with shock, the early morning traffic was horrible and I was driving at a good rate of speed merging onto the toll and I had to keep up with the flow and not stop until my exit, I had to keep cool as tears begin to fall from my eyes I asked her who it was and she begin to tell me, she begin to tell me the details as my stomach begin to burn, my heart was throbbing because she'd been begging me not to send her to daycare but she never gave me a good enough reason.

I immediately exited and went to my dad and fell on my knees with my baby in my arms and told him what had happened. He held me and my baby; he gave us a talk and told me I had to go to the family member's parents (because the family member that touched her was a minor as well yet old enough to know what he was doing). I pulled myself together; she pulled herself together and wanted to go to school although I didn't want her to.

She went to school and I went to work, still angry, confused, hurt, feeling guilty and not knowing what to do next. I realized I had to pull myself together and made the phone call to the family member and told her we needed to talk and it was urgent; she came to me and we talked and it almost broke her down because she had a feeling something was wrong but again was unsure. I think from that day on, she began to have seizures, she was torn apart and I know some would say I should've done this and I should've done that. I prayed about it and we prayed about it together. I asked my daughter what she wanted me to do about it and she said she didn't want to hurt her aunt but he needed to get help. It took a minute but we dealt with it our own way, he didn't penetrate her and I had to give God the glory for that alone.

Here I am thinking this was the end and tried to make sense of my crazy life. Trying to figure out how I came from this street person that was wild and crazy to the tired naïve person that life seemed to be going crazy.

When M.T. got in I spoke to him about it and he was behind me with whatever decision I made and we prayed about it even though I was still yet angry.

With all the distractions going on and no attention on my oldest daughter she was starting to feel herself and made new friends in high school. She wanted to be with the high school crew and I even allowed some of them over to my house to hang out with her (I was always the mom that everyone wanted to hang around, even with my strict rules, the kids was able to talk to me on a serious note – I was always good at talking to young people and helping them through so much because of all that I'd been through). My daughter's friends would come around and they liked sitting around talking to M.T. as well, until I found out that M.T. was talking to them about sex and making sure that they don't let men get over on them.

Yeah you're saying "what's wrong with that"! Well that wasn't the big issue because that was a good thing, the issue was, he was also talking to them about if they do have sex, that they need to be careful of the different sizes of men, how it would feel being as they were all virgins, so many spirits being leaked into their spirit. I went to him again and told him he wasn't allowed to talk to the girls and again he used the excuse that it was stuff they needed to know because they got so comfortable talking to him, they shared that they was having the desire to have sex, so he was preparing them.

I begin at that time to really seek the face of God for direction in my life. I needed to know from God if I was just over reacting because he wasn't their biological father, how would I act if it was their own father, would I take it that serious, I was just going in circles mentally.

Not long after that Taja started sneaking out the house, running away and just doing all kinds of crazy things. I was calling the police and still just lost in a world wind, but I never ceased from praying, because praying was all I had left to do, I was still so tired from the years of being neglected as a child, then the abuse and felt I was still a hostage in another man's cage (the cave of life).

Not many months after my oldest daughter was pulling all of her stunts, she ended up pregnant at the age of 16 and I wanted to lay down and die, my heart was so torn and tired until I wanted to give up but giving up really hasn't been an option for me. I stayed on the battlefield while God was showing me that my oldest daughter was just trying to find herself, she'd lost her childhood during the abuse when she had to be an adult at a young age. We cried but of course I had to have her back, she was my baby and I couldn't turn my back on her. Only to go to the doctors and find out she was pregnant with twins but there was nothing we could do, abortion wasn't even in our vocabulary, so we had to prepare our lives for twins (I think I was excited a little☺).

I was still so exhausted within, mentally and emotionally, because I'd never really gotten a break from the other drama in my life, it's always been one thing after another for me. I felt like I was born to hurt, so that I can minister to other people when they are hurt in the same area. I've always told my god sister that and my Pastor. I would get angry and say *"God, why was I born, did you create me to be the one that carry hurt, go through it and minister it to other people for their deliverance"*, one day my Pastor said *"yes it's possible"* I'm like ARE YOU SERIOUS, what do you mean possible…he explained to me that I was called and that I was chosen, that God had appointed me and anointed me for these trials, he said Yolanda, God has said *"Consider my servant Yolanda"! MANY ARE CALLED BUT FEW ARE CHOSEN Matthew 22:14* he said you are called and chosen, consider yourself blessed that God would even use you to carry burdens for HIS glory. In my mind, I'm like *"are you crazy, do you hear yourself telling me to consider that a blessing to go through pure hell all the time just for someone else, you have to be kidding me"*. Well well well, God is faithful and HE is just, so I won't complain.

Chapter 5 ~ There's a stranger in the house "What is my radar picking up!"

As time went on, I was doing speaking for different groups mainly Bay Area Legal Service, so I started a support group called "Bethany's Group" for families in Domestic Violence and had to leave out for speaking on Saturday's, but I'd wake up, go to early morning prayer, come back, change clothes and head to my events; but I noticed that my middle daughter would always be awake when I came home sitting on the couch next to M.T. and I'd always say to her "what are you doing woke, you normally sleep all day" and he'd intervene and say "oh she wanted to wake up and read the bible", that put a smile on my face but at the same time, it put a question mark in my head *"wow Tae wanna learn the bible, well that's a good thing though".*

I felt if something negative was going on, my daughter would now tell me being as she went through this already with a family member and again, I've always talk to my kids about people touching them and making sure they tell me and I'd deal with it and they assured me AGAIN they would tell me, especially after this situation Tae had already been through. **There's a Stranger in my house!**

So it was time for our normal talks (something I did with them as a family) and I sat them down, asked if everything was ok, was there anything we need to discuss and as always I asked them if anyone had been touching them or tried to, this is a talk I gave all 5 of my kids, each of them assured me that nothing was wrong. Every now and then Tae would ask what would I do if someone touched them/her again and I told her I'd kill them, she'd say but you go to prison and I'd tell her I didn't care about that as long as the person who touched them was dead. Now right there, parents would cheer that on saying **"I KNOW THAT'S RIGHT"**, but to a child, this kid is saying *"man if momma/daddy kill this person, they go to prison – all we have is her/him, so if they go to prison, who will take care of us"*. You see I didn't know that was a child's way of thinking at the time and because of that thinking, it kept my child (ren) from telling me things – as I later in life learned.

My oldest daughter Taja started getting bigger and I knew the babies would be here soon. I didn't want to raise my grandbabies in a house with stairs in them so I prepared to move and being as our church was in Town N' Country I decided we'd get a house in that area. M.T. decided to buy but I didn't want my name on the house. My god-sister kept asking why wouldn't I want my name on the house with my husband, I told her it was just something in my spirit telling me not to put my name on that house.

When we moved into the new house, I kept all my boxes and M.T. asked why I kept my boxes and I told him it was just something I felt I wanted to keep. I didn't realize God was preparing my storage.

My family was about to grow bigger so M.T. felt I needed at truck (he knew that was my dream - to one day have a truck) so he took me one Saturday morning and put the money down on me a truck and I got a white Yukon for my family.

Time continued to go on and I noticed that Tae had this certain anger about her, I also notice M.T. did more for her than the others but he fussed at her more than the others and I went to him about it and he claimed the others didn't ask for anything and that Tae always asked so she got it. I went to Tae again and asked if someone's been touching her and she said no, but I was still uneasy, something in my spirit kept saying something is very wrong but I couldn't put my hands on it and Tae kept saying nothing was wrong. *There was a Stranger in my house!*

One day I called her into my room and asked her to please tell me if M.T. or anyone had been touching her because I was picking up things in my spirit that I didn't like and she assured me. I went to M.T. and I said I'm picking up some real bad spirits and I don't like them and I've asked my kids if you've ever said anything or touched them in any way that you shouldn't; he got upset and asked how could I do something like that and I told him I was feeling uneasy and that something was wrong but he assure me that nothing was wrong and that he'd never do that to a child and I needed to seek God for forgiveness for thinking he'd do something like that, because God knew he wasn't like that. He always used God in every conversation. ***There's a Stranger in my house!***

CHAPTER 6 ~MOMA DON'T KILL HIM
"The Prayers of the Righteous"

I continued to pray and seek the face of God! Well it was family night again and we always ask the kids if they had questions and Tae said *"momma if someone say they are a Christian but they touch kids, will God kill them"* and I said to her, I don't know about God but I know I will if it's my kids, but why are you asking that question all the time now and she said again, *no reason ma I just asked*...I said to her, you are lying to me and I said out loud to her, is M.T. or anyone touching you and he yelled out, why would you ask that, I would never do that and God knows I wouldn't and Tae yelled out "no ma no one is touching me, I just asked". It continued to burn in my spirit as if I was literally on fire inside and I continued to pray.

We went to church that Sunday and the Pastor and his wife said they needed to have a meeting with me after church and I said ok. After church I went and met with them and they begin to tell me that Tae told her in Sunday School that she'd been experiencing kisses and being touched by a boy in school, that this little boy had tried to penetrate her but it didn't work, by this time M.T. walks in; but the story that Tae had given them didn't sound right because she wasn't able to do that kind of activity in elementary school that she was at because for the most part, the teachers where with them when they weren't in the class room, bottom line, it just didn't sound real and I told my Pastor that I'd get to the bottom of it because the story didn't sound right and he agreed. Yet we didn't understand why she would make that up and tell it to the Pastor's wife, but M.T. was there saying we'd get to the bottom of it and no one better not have touched her but I noticed Tae's blank stare.

Again I lay before God asking him to please reveal what was going on in my house. That night M.T. and I talked and he told me we needed to go on a fast and see what God shows us and I agreed so we went to bed. With him saying this, it had me confused, "he can't be doing anything asking me to go on a fast because this dude knows that I'm anointed and God WILL reveal to me in due season and I think the season was about up"; so either dude is trying to really mess my head up and block my hearing from God OR he's really not doing anything and want to get to the bottom of it so that we can live and I not be so tensed with him.

As time went on my Taja had her babies, the babies was in the hospital maybe a week or so (the stayed in the hospital longer due to being born premature and their weight was low) and finally came home. We begin to enjoy the life of the babies, had them dedicated back to the Lord by our Pastor and M.T. took a lot of time out playing with the boys and helping us with them when he was there. Tae got attached to the babies and just loved them up and she surrounded herself with playing with the babies and wanting to be a part of them.

M.T. came in on a Friday as usual, we had dinner and it was time for bed. M.T. was lying next to me in the bed and when I rolled over God showed me the face of a snake instead of M.T. face and I jumped, I stayed up all night and prayed and every time I looked at M.T. while he slept it was the face of a snake (no I wasn't scared, I was walking now in the realm of the spirit, God was working something out and I had no time for fear).

That Sunday evening he left for his truck routes for the week and he returned on Friday as always. When he returned Friday we did our usual eat, pray and talk. Later that night M.T. wanted to make love to me and that was fine he'd been gone and that was my job as his wife. While M.T. was on top of me and got ready to kiss me I saw that snake coming down at my face and I screamed and told him he needed to get off me and get off me now. He jumped up and tried to hold me, asking me repeatedly what was wrong but I couldn't tell him, I thought I was going crazy in my flesh but I knew in my spirit, God was showing me something.

I pulled myself together and I fell on my face again and begged God to show me what was wrong. That Saturday morning I went for early morning prayer, which normally starts at 6am but I waited until it was over because I needed to go lay on my face at the altar before God with no interruptions and I needed to hear clearly what God had to say to me. I saw the First lady of the church and told her that I needed to pray and I wanted to pray alone, so she made it clear that no one was to bother me. I fell on my face at the altar and I cried out to God to show me what was going on, I told the Lord something was going on in my house and I needed to know, that my daughter was being touched and I needed an answer, but the Lord didn't say anything to me (just because God is quiet doesn't mean HE is not at work. *Pastor Laytecia McKinney says "Learn to trust Him even when you can't trace Him"*). I wasn't there long, maybe 30 minutes because I was grinding in the spirit realm and I needed a right now God for a right now situation (how many know when the situation get intense, so does your cry unto God IF YOU HAVE A PRAYER LIFE and/or a relationship with God).

I got up and went home and planned on going out for a while with the kids to see Mother Ferguson. When I got home I told Taja to get the twins ready, and told Tae to get ready as I prepared Jr and Navia to leave the house. M.T. was in the other room studying the bible, which was his normal routine.

He begin to fuss at Tae for some stranger reason telling her to do something crazy that I can't even remember, Tae told him to leave her alone and my kids know I didn't allow disrespect from them in any way to an adult. So it shocked me and I said to her "Tae you know I don't play that disrespect what is your problem", M.T. then yelled out that she's grown (which reminded me of when my ex-husband hit my other daughter in the face and told her she was grown and acting like me) and she continued to talk back and for the life of me I didn't understand what was going on inside her, "where this rage was coming from, why she was being disrespectful after I had already told her to shut it down", at this time I was sitting at my computer desk with both twins at my feet in their car seat, but the Lord instructed me at that time to keep quiet and be still because I was about to snatch her up but on the other hand, I knew that something was very wrong for her to still be going on. (SEE GOD WAS QUIET EARLIER, BUT NOW HE'S SPEAKING TO ME QUIETLY IN THE SPIRIT REALM) M.T. went on to tell her that if she keep talking smart he'd give her a spanking and she said to him, **know you're not going to touch me** (although I wasn't going to allow him to spank my child, I remained quiet as God had instructed me to do), he went into the room as if he was going to spank her and I said to him, "I hope you know you're not going to touch my child", he walked in the room and she screamed out, *"I DARE YOU TO TOUCH ME, IF YOU COME ANYWHERE NEAR ME I'LL TELL MY MOM WHAT YOU'VE BEEN DOING TO ME ALL THIS TIME"*, I immediately sat straight up (my gun was sitting next to me in my bag because I never went anywhere without it) and I called to Tae and she didn't come, *(I realize right now some of you are saying, heck naw, it couldn't have been you, I'm crazy, he was supposed to die, yadda yadda yadda, but I was and still am a child that's very obedient to the voice of God, (especially when GOD speaks in the tone that HE had spoken in),* I wasn't going to deviate for my flesh, later you'll see why listening to God was so important as some of you need to start doing)

M.T. came running out the room yelling *"baby don't believe anything she says, she just don't like me and don't want us to be happy, she knows that you will try to kill me or leave me if she tell you this mess"*, I said to M.T., PLEASE don't talk and I put my finger up to my lips in the hush motion and I got up because I wanted to get a better understanding to what my child had just said and wanted to be sure my ears didn't just deceive me, especially after asking her this for so long and she denied it. **PLEASE UNDERSTAND I WAS NO LONGER WALKING IN THE**

FLESH BUT EVERYTHING WAS MOVING IN THE SPIRIT REALM, it literally seemed as if everything was moving in slow motion.

I walked into her room as she began to cry, she fell against the wall and slid to the floor saying *"momma I'm so sorry, I been wanted to tell you but you seemed so happy for the first time in your life and I didn't want to take your happiness, ma you've been through so much and I didn't want to hurt you any more"*, I immediately ran back out the room and went for my gun, all the children was standing there and Taja said to me *"momma please don't, if you kill him we won't have anyone, all we have is you, where would we go"*, Tae begin to cry asking me to please don't do it because they needed me, I went to my knees asking God what to do and I immediately called my Pastor with the gun still in my hands and he being to pray and told me to please leave the house with the kids. By this time M.T. had run back into the other room still saying "please believe me, asks God and he'll tell you the truth", which enraged me more because that means, *"you're literally just going to sit and play with God in my face like this"*. My baby Tae begins to scream, *"You touched me, you touched me and then you'd go read the bible, I hate you, you're not a man of God you're a fake"*. My children were still screaming and crying and Taja had gotten the twins and said momma what will I do with them without you, I was still on the phone with the Pastor and I begin to slowly walk away because Taja placed one of the twins in my arms. I left the house with my kids and went to my Pastor as he'd requested of me. After I pulled it together, we spoke further with Tae, I needed to assure to my baby that NOTHING and NO ONE came before them but God.

The Pastor called our Bishop and he called a personal friend from DCF. The person instructed me to find out from my daughter if she'd be penetrated and because this was a Saturday if they came out, unfortunately they'd take all of my children out of the house until they investigated and because I'd never been through that I didn't know what to do. She instructed me to try and hold off until he left on Sunday (I explained to her that he leaves out on Sunday's after church). I didn't want my children to be taken (she explained why this would happen). So I did as I was told by the person from DCF, my daughter said he'd never went inside her but it was hard for me to believe her now because she hadn't told me the truth about the entire situation. Yet the person from DCF told me I had a choice, to either go through with the report or wait until the next day when I knew that he'd be leaving out to go on the trucks. So I decided to wait, which meant that my Pastor, my Bishop and I had to hold our peace and I had to go back to the house hours later with my children and wait on him to leave on the truck on Sunday.

I asked my children how they felt about having to go back and had to promise them I wouldn't kill him because they again begged me to not leave them by killing him. They assured me that they would be fine and that they didn't mind going back to the house. The two younger kids were there but wasn't 100% sure what was really going on. So we made it back to the house M.T. was sitting in the very back of the house with the bible open reading it, I wanted so bad to blow his brains out right in front of my kids (being obedient to God isn't always easy, so don't get me wrong and think it was just so easy to do, like I'm just so super spiritual and sold out for God and nothing could get to me; everything in me wanted to do the opposite but I knew my kids needed me more than allowing my flesh to consume me and I knew that **NOT** listening to God and doing it HIS way would cost me more than I was willing to give up).

We got home, I fed my kids, prayed with my kids, showered and the kids and I went to bed. M.T. stayed up front for a long time until after he thought I was asleep and of course I didn't sleep all night, I cried my night away because I wanted to kill him so badly, I wanted to literally slit his throat, no longer shoot him, but if I shot him I wanted to shoot him between his legs or cut it off. My mind wondered all night and because he was afraid, I can feel he didn't sleep either.

I got up Sunday morning and prepared myself for church with my kids, we went to church and this man followed a little time later. He stood in the church and pretended to pray hard and I couldn't take it anymore and broke down in the church but no one knew what was going on but my Pastor and the first lady. Church was over and I went home with my kids and he went to his truck.

After he went to work the personal friend at DCF came to make the report and got an order to keep him from the house and issued a warrant for his arrest. They went to his job and he was already gone out on the truck long distance, so they had to wait until he returned. During this time my daughter went through hell and high water. She being to go into a depression because she felt she took my happiness away, she felt like after all I'd been through, I was finally happy and she took that by telling, she felt like now I'd be lonely again (which was far from the truth). I assured my baby that my happiness was with my children, a man come a dime a dozen and **NO MAN** was going to come before them and I already felt it in my spirit. **I DON'T UNDERSTAND WHY SOME WOMEN LOVE THE MAN MORE THAN THEIR CHILD THAT'S BEING MOLESTED.**

Later that night I called my baby into my room and she sat on the bed, I asked her to talk to me and tell me what really happened. It was hard for her to tell me everything and it was even harder for me to listen to it. He didn't penetrate her but she said she knew she had to tell me soon because he kept trying and got to the point he was begging her to let him go inside of her, that he'd tried but it wouldn't go in.

I couldn't hear anymore, I felt my stomach tighten and I wanted to vomit and I wanted to kill him. She said it all started when she stayed home from school sick and went out on the trucks with him, she said that day he said he just wanted to teach her how to kiss, she said she was afraid and she didn't want to tell me because I always told her that I would kill anyone that touched them and she didn't want me to leave them. **(Lesson learned)** *I learned a valuable lesson at that very moment on telling them what I'd do instead of assuring them that it was ok for her to tell me and I'd deal with it my own way.*

I realize it's in a parent (guardian's nature) to want to kill someone if they touch your child (ren) but you have to be careful telling that to the child, especially if you're the sole provider, if that child feels like you will kill for them, but yet leave them, they will be hesitant on telling you if they've been violated out of fear of losing the only person they love and/or love them. We must assure our children that it's ok to tell you, without telling them what you'll do. Just assure them that you'll handle it.

Chapter 7 ~ Obeying the Voice of God

The police left a message at M.T.'s job that he needed to contact them. During this process my family was twisted and turned once again. My family had to be interviewed by DCF, questioned etc. to make sure he didn't touch any of the other kids, Tae had to be taken to a gynecologist to make sure she'd actually not been penetrated (although she insisted she wasn't penetrated, they needed to make sure that she wasn't saying no out of fear), so here she is just a little girl having to be touched and probed all because of another grown man's insane spirit. Here's a child getting a pep (which her doctor did not want to give her but she had to by law for the report).

I'm thankful that we had a wonderful female doctor and she was very gentle with my baby. She was found not to have been penetrated (PRAISE GOD) and the report was giving to DCF. She went through so much because DCF had to come to her school and do more questioning and it was just hard on all the kids.

M.T. did immediately come back into the truck yard and went to the police department as directed. They took him in and they questioned him, gave him a lie detectors test and he passed it. They weren't allowed to tell me the questions that they asked him but they did tell me that lie detectors are not 100% accurate but because of the fact he passed it there was nothing they could do, it was her word against his. The detectives came out and told me that at this time they could only keep it on file but they couldn't actually put charges on him. One guy secretly told me that the questions they asked "anyone could pass and get away with it", he said it all depends on the questions and how calm the person remains.

I was devastated and wondered if I made the right decision not to blast him, but I knew I made the right decision because who would be there for my children, who would be going through all of this backlash with my children? NO ONE that we can think of that would really care or care for them like a mother would, so I needed to be there for them. They helped put my daughter in counseling and Bay Area Legal Services got me a divorce effective immediately. *The detective praised me for not shooting M.T. because he said, due to the findings, if I'd shot him, I would have gone to jail for shooting him. They said because he didn't penetrate her, it was her word against his word and that's all they could go by.* They said there are many women in prison (and father's) for shooting someone because of things such as this and even domestic violence, but without certain proof, the person who did the crime always seems to walk.

So by listening to God, my Pastor and my children, I know I made the right decision in not allowing my flesh to kill him, because if I had killed him, my kids would be alone without me and I'd be in prison. Not knowing what affect that would've had on my kids and especially Tae because she felt it was her fault that all this happened and that I no longer had happiness. My children are my happiness!

Chapter 8 ~ Where do we go from here?

I got an injunction on M.T. so that he could no longer come to the house, he came with the police to get his clothes, I signed papers to move out of the house so that we could move on with our lives and start over yet again because I didn't want the house or anything attached to him, we had no children together so I knew once I walked away, I'd NEVER have to see him again. AND I still had all my boxes to pack (thank you Lord for speaking to me to keep my boxes).

Due to the fact our church was in the same area we lived in, we wanted to stay in that area in order not to have to drive so far from the house, so we found a duplex not far from the house we lived in. I prepared to get rid of the truck that I had with M.T. and get other transportation. M.T. didn't want the house either and he never came back to it, he signed all the papers to forfeit the house and not get any money from it, just a clean sell that would cover the unpaid expenses etc.

So again it was time we started putting our pieces back together yet again. Tae was still in a depressed mode and I had to assure her that I loved her and that it was ok. I was happier with my children than I was with any man. We continued to go to church, my church family (those that knew what was going on) stood firm with us and prayed us through some hard times yet again.

After time went on, my oldest daughter Taja was somewhat exhausted with life, losing her youth to seeing the abuse for 10 ½ yrs., running, hiding and helping me with the kids, having a nervous breakdown herself, then thinking she was able to breath, she started going wild, gets pregnant with twins, have them, M.T. molesting her sister right after the twins are born, it became too much and she felt she needed a way of escape and she needed to get away. She ended up going to Jacksonville for a little while with one of her friends, coming back and forth to spend time with the twins. I didn't give her a hard time about her decision, she was young and I understood.

Many days I cried quietly wishing I could just run away too because I'd lived such a rollercoaster life all of my life. Tae got to where she smothered herself around the twins and that was her new project...making sure the twins was tended to.

Tae slowly started to see that I loved her no matter what, but other spirits begin to raise its head within Tae, I tried really hard to ignore that spirit but it was obvious. We'd been through so much I was so exhausted mentally, emotionally and physically but I had to keep pressing, I was all they had and I couldn't fail them, they'd been let down and failed for a very long time.

The little place that we'd moved into was very small and we quickly out grew it and I was trying to figure out where we'd go next, still not wanting to leave the area of the church.

During all this time, I'd been in contact with a longtime family friend (we'll call him Victor for name sake) that was in federal prison via phone and letters. For the most part Victor helped keep me sane through all of this madness because he understood, and again, we were nothing more than friends. I'd known him since I was a little girl in elementary school; he hung with my brother growing up, my family knew his family and he'd been to my parents' house and vice versa.

We did have a run in a few times while I was wilding in the streets; he was a big drug dealer (that's why he was in prison). I would always tell him what was going on and he always gave me something positive to go on and I felt safe because he was there in prison and I was home and it wasn't sexual.

Time had gone by and it Victor was coming home to work release, my sister and I decided we'd go pick him up from prison and take him to the center (remember he's a family friend, not an outside new friend, he was like a adopted brother in the house).

So my sister and I took out that morning headed to South Carolina, we had so much fun on the drive there and back. Victor and I still remained friends and I helped him out in every way that I could when he got to the center. I helped him get on his feet, for the most part with clothes and a vehicle. He met the kids and they loved him, especially the twins because they were still just babies. Tae took to him and it shocked me because I thought she would have a fear of men, but he was more like a family member because my parents always knew him, and again he did dirt with my brother, so he wasn't a stranger to any of us. He came in showing genuine care for Tae because he knew what had happened to her and what all my children had gone through in general, but I was still protective and watchful of everyone that came around them now.

I thought I was over protective before but this time I was overboard, I wasn't taking any more chances and I didn't care if it was male or female.

Victor started going to church with us and it was nice having him around when he wasn't at the center, Tae was able to talk to him when she didn't want to talk to me, especially about this new spirit that was about to surface.

Chapter 9~ Lord I see more demons ahead.

Since the space we were living in had grown small, I found another place around the corner with a pool and we moved into it. Not long after we moved I was starting to see a stronger spirit that was forming in Tae, it appeared that Tae was unsure what to do with herself, she wasn't sure which way to turn because she'd been molested physically and mentally twice, now her little spirit has been molested within because she trusted the family member and the so-called *man of God in the church,* so that really had her twisted. She didn't hate men/ men of God because even to this day she loves our Pastor and our Bishop, she doesn't judge all men for the wrong that M.T. did to her, although she doesn't trust men in any fashion and she don't want a man around her to much other than immediate family. One minute Tae was dressing like a sleaze, she was wearing clothes too little for her and tight, then the next minute she was dressing in big clothes like a boy, then finally she geared towards dressing more like a boy. She wanted to cover her body up and not allow anyone to see her body. She was feeling like the normal person would feel **"MOMMA WHY ME"** and I didn't have an answer for her as much as I wish I did. (I did find that quite a bit of children that have been molested, they either become promiscuous or gay). Nevertheless, I mentioned to Victor what spirit I was seeing and feeling was taking control of Tae and he said he'd watch. I went to my Pastor and the first lady and told them and they begin to watch and pray with me as well.

When we'd be at church, Victor would come in a separate car and the kids always wanted to leave with him because he'd always stop and buy them junk or pizza so that was fun for them. Victor must have taken the opportunity to talk to Tae in regards to my assumptions and she confided in him and obviously asked him to help her talk to me. By now Victor is out of the work release center and we've started a small relationship, I say small because I was still vulnerable and wasn't ready for a relationship with anyone although Victor and I grew up around each other and had been family friends since Elementary school.

Victor comes over one night and Tae runs outside and talk to him, she comes back into the house, then Victor calls me outside, he then proceeds to tell me that Tae has told him that she likes women and want to be gay. When he told me that, I refused to listen, although deep within I already knew it, but I didn't want it to be true. Victor asked me to be still and just listen; he called Tae outside to talk to me directly and I bluntly told her I didn't want to hear it, I refuse to accept it and to get out of my face and I walked away. Victor came into the house and tried to talk to me and told me not to shut her out. I wasn't shutting HER out but I wasn't accepting that crap about being gay because it's a **SPIRIT**.

We didn't talk about it anymore but Tae started to slowly rebel against authority. Taja moved back home after getting in some trouble and my life was still full. Tae started running away and hiding, I'd make police reports, I'd go look for her and Victor would always talk to her and she'd listen for a little while. She was an excellent basketball player so she started playing for the school, she was so good Plant High School came out to see her and wanted her to play for them when she went to High School that following year.

Tae was being so rebellious on and off until she didn't make it to High School because she kept running away. When I went to get her again, she told me she hated me, she wished that I'd stop looking for her and sending the police to find her, to just go and leave her alone. I was tired, my mind was in a world wind, I'd been through so much and I just wanted to let go of everything that was going on within me and run away. I pulled myself together and I let her go. I prayed about it and asked God to please help me, I felt like I was having another break down...I was exhausted with everything I'd been through. I made the decision to let her go physically, continue to watch over her spiritually and be there when she needed me. I laid on my face day in and day out asking God to cover her and it was hard. Victor stood by me and tried to comfort me but in the midst of it all, Victor didn't really know my pain. Victor always had things handed to him or he made things happen, he'd never experienced anything like that before so he couldn't relate. I continued to move forward and do the best I can to continue raising the other kids and grandkids.

Taja was back being helpful as always, but things was still nerve racking for her too, she still needed so much healing and it bothered her to see Tae act out on me like that but, she also saw the reality of some of what she took me through. She saw the hurt in my eyes, the pain of knowing I felt like I was a failure and the reality of ***"this is what I did to my mom as well"***, so Taja wanted to do better and be helpful to me but it didn't last long with her being around, she still wasn't healed/delivered so she was working on the surface of life as always after all we'd been through.

Through all of this madness, I still went to work full-time, still participated with the other kids schooling, still dealt with daycare for the twins and not long after all that Taja moved out and went to live with her grandmother. I was still too strict, I wasn't allowing any and everything to go on in front of the other two kids and the twins, my rules were still standing in my house. Taja still made sure she did what she could when it came to the twins. Victor and I were still dating.

Chapter 10 ~ Picking up the pieces and moving on!

Driving from Town n' Country to West Tampa two and three times a day was starting to be too much for me, the expense was too much as well, so I moved closer to West Tampa to make it easier on myself. I was seeing Tae a lot, taking food to where she was living, making sure she had everything she needed, I got her a phone and was paying her bill in order that I can stay in contact with her. It was hard but I had to let her go in order for her to learn her lesson and it was hurting me daily and I didn't want her to hate me more or run and I not know where she was. So it was the twins, Jr and Nae, just the 4 of us making it work and Victor when he came over. I was still drained but I'd learned how to stay at the feet of the ROCK which is Jesus. I'd learned how to cast my cares upon the Lord and lean not to my own understand but in all my ways, acknowledge God. NO it wasn't easy, it was very hard but I had to pull myself together and go forward with the help of God for the sake of myself, my children and my grandchildren. Tae was back in counseling but it was still too much for her, she still wasn't at a place of releasing. Outside of that, I started to see that in her counseling sessions, there were other hurting girls that had been molested fully, they'd been completely violated by their mothers boyfriends, their fathers, brother etc. and some of them were made to feel it was their fault by the parent and some was gay and some was pernicious. It still was bad spirits for Tae to be around because those spirits were in agreement with one another, so once she no longer wanted to go, it was yet well with my soul because this matter needed counsel from God, not from the ungodly counsel Amen!

Nevertheless, we all begin to deal with the hurts, mistakes and all that had taken place in our lives, Tae still came around and some nights she'd stay over and that was well with my soul also.

I didn't put a lot into Part III as some thought that I would, Part III was a hurting reminder, more than Part II with the abuse of me. I can handle my own personal hurt but when the violation came directly at my daughter and I had to relive it by writing this book (with her permission), it was hard. Although I've healed some, I don't think I'll ever stop feeling the cringe in my flesh, mind, body and soul when I think about what he did to my baby and had her doing to him. She's still in so much pain and I deal with it secretly such as she does because I'm angry with myself. I am yet grateful that God didn't allow him to penetrate her and I do know that what the devil think that he's attached to my baby for bad, God is already about to turn this thing around for her good. I still believe her being gay is just temporal☺. God is faithful and HE is just to do just what HE said.

Yet I do know *"THIS TOO SHALL PASS"*

The End of Part III

SIDE~BARS!

This book is not about following our lives, it's about showing you all that no matter what you may go through, you keep your faith and know that God is still faithful and HE is just. **Jeremiah 1:5** *Before I formed thee in the belly I knew thee; and before thou camest forth out of the womb I sanctified thee, and I ordained thee a prophet unto the nations.* I'm going to end here because there's so much work left to do, so many unspoken chapters that need to surface. Before I close I'll let Tae share a brief in her own words of her story that's still hard for me to read a reality that still haunts our family till this very day.

First read a poem by my book designer: Ronika Hughes

Poem By: Ronika Hughes

It's a question I always seemed to ask myself...dealing with this life I've lived undetected like stealth. Walking round head down eyes low to the ground thinking people would never find out, about the way I live, late nights in the club looking for a man to love, stripping just to make a dub, crying myself to sleep at night wondering why my life was filled with hate and strife You're right I wanna change but it's gotta start with me first, let me switch this round don't wanna end up in a black hearse, It's time to stop and think about what I've done...I've disrespected the Son I've disrespected the one who gave me life every day that I opened my eyes to sunrise, bird's chirping, my should don't even know it but it's hurting...I need you now, I need ya now...Just tell me why?

> Tell me why I'm going through this pain and why there's so much rain inside
> Tell me why sometimes I feel like I just wanna die and all that I can do is cry
> Tell me why, why I'm feeling so alone taking this world all on my own, Tell me why? Tell me why?

I'm crying out to you asking for forgiveness from all the things I've done all the things committed against your will what's' my purpose I have no idea, why I'm still here, every night I cry out, but to whom was I calling on praying for help it wasn't God that I was calling on praying for strength I had my trust in man never understood your plan but always got knocked down, smiles turned to frowns and every time I looked around all I seen was pain, why do I go through this mess trying hard to maintain, my sanity, my composure, my life is getting closer to falling in to a million pieces their broken, I'm tryna get it together but someone has a remote, their pushing buttons, changing channels, yo my life was a joke looking for my childhood but ain't no turning back I gotta do what I can cause they ain't giving no slack. I pop a pill to ease the pain, I try to go on and maintain, thoughts is moving faster than my brain, am I insane, somebody tell me why?

Tell me why I'm going through this pain and why there's so much rain inside
Tell me why sometimes I feel like I just wanna die and all that I can do is cry
Tell me why, why I'm feeling so alone taking this world all on my own, Tell me why? Tell me why?

It's over grab a hold of Jehovah now, no more feelings of loneliness guilt or shame He will always be your sunshine through the rain, it ain't always peaches and cream but best believe you can get through the strain with ease, is your faith the size of a mustard seed, that all I need babygirl and to drop to my knees and give Him thanks cause he showed me my destiny cause otherwise it could've been a straight tragedy, left alone in a room bullet shot to the chest , cried out to HIM and gave up the rest, you can't have a testimony without the test, so stand strong lil mama God's got ya hand, never put your trust in man and just stick to the plan, keep your head up high and keep your eyes on the prize I Thank God cause he saved my life.

"Excerpt from Tae's story"

(names have been changed for personal protection)

It was summer time school was out and the end was just the beginning. We had just moved to Valrico from hell being with my father. Moving on to a better life. things were going good for us finally, now there's this deacon in the church name M.T., he was a cool dude we all liked him my mom did a lot and it was a plus cause he was in the church an always was there for us when we were going through it with my dad, he drove trucks played with us an all he was the perfect step dad jus strict but he was alright with me and things were going good him an my mom started talking an seeing each other more until he moved right on in. The house in Valrico was one of the best houses he had was going to Mulrannan middle school with my cousins Ray~Ray and Life was finally how it should be my mom's happy we are just living life. Mr. M.T. sure brought comfort to our hearts. We drove on his truck sometimes it had a big bed in it just in case he rode out of town. I even road a couple times on my own oh did I enjoy it being in a truck so big and remember when I use to do the choo choo thing with my arm watching other truck's pass by an now I'm finally in one. things at home was just how it should be my dad finally away my mom was doing better my siblings were getting big I was myself boy the good days I say...to see my mom as happy as she was joy to my heart I wouldn't mess that up for nothing can trust I meant what I said when I thought about it to myself...my mom was happy with this man. Mr. M.T. cleaned helped out with many things. Mr. M.T. had kids also they came over sometimes I liked them but me and my oldest sister Taja couldn't stand each other crazy huh; but back to the subject. Some of my funniest times were riding on the trucks hearing the engine roar and the loud horn and being able to see other trucks when we went to the flying J to fuel the truck up. The flying J had a whole restaurant in it we ate there a lot. it was a day when I was supposed to go with my stepdad tony to ride on the trucks by myself I got to eat whatever I wanted I had so many things in mind. On this particular night things didn't go as planned so I'm in the bed inside of the truck normal routine having a good time we get are food and head to the rest stop to eat a go to sleep to head home the next day. As I lay in the bed in the dark waiting for my body to drift off to sleep I feel a touch an him tell me it's okay I didn't understand but I knew what was being done wasn't right I was scared and didn't understand why he was doing this to me he was supposed to be better than this I really didn't understand things about God yet but I knew enough to know that if he was a man of god why would he do this to me. So as he continues to touch me in places I didn't like. My breast between my legs I hated when he stuck his finger in me because it always hurt I knew he wasn't supposed to touch me he began to rub his penis up against my butt I wanted to cry but if my mom could go through that and be strong I could to and I did just that stayed strong an prayed. The next morning he told me to not tell anybody he was way much older an bigger so I did as I was told when we got home he act as if nothing happened he kisses my mom an tells her hello I speak an go upstairs to my room scared and confused about the whole thing only comfort I had was doing my puzzle it was huge or hurt myself me thinking things were going to get better I was wrong things only got worse this was just the beginning to a troubled minded child (*silent screams of a child*) being turned into a monster as the days went all my feelings toward this man changed I hated him. I hated when my mom left me sleep at home when he was there because I didn't know if what was done once will be done again and it did as I thought it would. He would call me down to him and my mom's room I just wish I could have disappeared but it was impossible to do so I did as I was told as I push the door opened because my mom kept her door close as I walk into the room he tells me to come over to him I walked over scared he started rubbing and kissing me on my breast, neck, and mouth I was sick an felt like I was wrong at times thinking what did I do. Was it something I did to make him want to these things to me did I say something what did I do is all I could think about as he continued to touch me still I keep my mouth and eyes closed. He takes me into my mom's bathroom an sit me on the sink he pulls his penis out his pants and pulls my panties down he grabs his penis an rubs it up against my private area he had on his hulk pj's can't forget it. He attempted to insert his penis in me but he doesn't go all the way so he just rubes it around on my private I just wanted to die. When he stops I see white stuff come out the top of his penis not knowing what it was at the time, when I get off the sink he tells me again don't say anything (**SILENT SCREAMS OF A CHILD**) an I did as I was told seeing my mom as happy as she was I never wanted to mess it up an it be my fault so I kept my mouth close, I go up to my room and cry a began to hurt myself because I felt like if inflecting pain on me made him feel good maybe hurting myself would make me feel better also. My mom gets home and he again act's as if nothing happened. the day goes on and still I say nothing and I was the type of child if I try and tell someone something and they I don't want to say anything anymore I'm very sensitive so I kept it to myself. Days go by an every other day that I was left at home alone sleep he bothered with me same routine till when I hurt myself after the pain didn't bother me anymore my mind was on another level, still I say nothing, but check this the whole time my stepdad was bothering me I was attending my aunt daycare she had back then; well things were good there my cousin Ray-Ray was always with me and other kids, my aunt had a son named Joey he was like 16 or 17 maybe younger he was my sisters cousins but I called him mine to as well. One day as I lay facing the wall with my eyes closed ready to go to sleep because it was nap time at the time as I lay on the bed I feel a tap on my shoulder and who is it my cousin Joey taping me telling me to go in his room I still to this day member how his room was set up as I walk into his room he sits on the bed an tells me to come sit next to him. I'm thinking *"my god why me what did I do"* I started to hate god and I didn't believe he was real and all the prayer we was brought up in and this what happens to a child of God I didn't deserve what I got done to me, nobody does. As I sit on the bed next to him he starts to touch me in the same places Mr. M.T. did and this was my cousin not my real one but that's how I saw him now I see why he played a lil too much. Some from that day on he came and got me every day at the same time and I hated being there, but I really had no choice because my mom had to work. Every day he would touch me and kiss me and would tell me not to say anything. My cousin Ray Ray used to sleep in the bed across from me and my cousin Joey. I thought she was sleep every time he came and got me but after a while I realized she wasn't and that she knew each time. I remember he use to put porn on and make me watch it while he touch me and kiss me or while he get on top of me and act as if he was having sex with me like the porn that was on the TV. I felt so lost and scared but most of all I felt sick to my stomach. I just wanted God to tell me what I did wrong to make people wanna hurt me; was it because I was to quiet or was it because God didn't love me like I thought he did.

    I didn't know what to think or do because he would say don't tell or he would hurt me and at the time my aunt was strict so telling her scared me. So as the weeks and days went by I notice that some days he didn't bother me, but I didn't think nothing of it, I was just glad he was leaving me alone. Until one day I seen him waking my cousin Ray Ray up and I wondered if he was doing to her, what he'd been doing to me. I found out that he was doing the same exact things to her and neither of us was able to understand why and we both were afraid to tell. Some things I would rather keep to myself then be so open about, with all that I saw or done.

    As I look back on all of this, it has made me strong; I learned the evil loves to prey on the weak and silent people. We felt like telling wouldn't help us at all because Ray Ray felt that she wasn't liked by the family member anyways so it really wouldn't matter or that she would be blamed for what he was doing to her. She felt as if no one in that house would listen to her because she was an outsider from the beginning.

I feel like my personality kept me from telling on Joey and M.T. because I was kind of timid. Every time I got up the courage to tell, I would get (what I called) my feelings hurt so I never said anything until months later. I say get my feelings hurt because I would go to my mom and say "mom can I tell you something without you getting upset, and she'd say yes, but I'd hesitate and keep saying never mind and that made her mad and she'd tell me to leave her alone until I'm ready to tell her for real (not knowing how serious it was). So as time went on, I would try it again and the same things would happen and with me being as sensitive as I was and still is, I just shut down again, my relief has always been knitting and puzzles of Scooby doo. I still felt that God didn't love me at all. I started to have a hatred for men that was like a burning inside of me.

Well one day my mom was driving us to school and I asked the question again "ma can I tell you something and you won't get mad", she kinda brushed it and said "yeah Tae, what is it". I just blurted it out "JOEL'S BEEN TOUCHING ME AND DOING THINGS TO ME and RAY`RAY. I thought she was going to flip the car because she was on the interstate and I was so scared of what was next. If

I wasn't so sensitive to a raised voice I would've told her a long time ago, if I would've just said something instead of closing in and walking away.

My mom cried like you wouldn't believe (as she was still driving). She asked WHY didn't you tell me this when it first happened and I explained to her because he already had a problem, I didn't want anything to happen to him and just wanted him to stop and make it go away. My mom dropped my sister off to school and took me to my grandfather's house and told him what happened, my mom wanted to call the police but I just wanted it all to go away because I didn't want the other family members getting in trouble because of what he did. My grandpa held me and told me it was going to be ok, talked to me to make sure he never went inside of me and my mom said she'd handle it from there. My mom dealt with it and she made me a part of every decision and as a family we all handled it together. Today I can tolerate him but I still think about it every now and then and especially when he comes around the family and acts as if nothing has ever happened, yes some may say "girl he was young, let that go" but his age didn't give him the right to violate me and I really don't care who think I should let it go HE VIOLATED ME and he was wrong but to God be the glory! We moved from Valrico to Town N' Country and I thought MAYBE our lives would change and M.T. would stop touching me but I was wrong. We got back in church with my god-sisters and my god-mommy and they became my get away. I wanted to go spend the night with them all the time just to get away from the darkness at home with him, so whenever my mom wouldn't let me go, I cried because that was my place of escape, but my mom had no idea what was going on or what I wanted to run away from.

One day he was yelling at me and by then I was at my boiling point, my mom always asked me if anyone else had bothered me, if M.T. had bothered me and I'd always so no because I was afraid yet again and I felt I would ruin my mom's happiness, she finally looked happy. So many times I wanted to tell my mom but this particular day I was boiling over and he said he would beat me. He had a feeling I was about to tell my mom because of the way he was raising his voice and I begin to raise mine, knowing my mom don't allow disrespect to adults…so finally I yelled it out to my mom, that he touches me and you're trying to beat me to keep me from telling. My mom jumped up and scream "WHAT DID YOU JUST SAY" and I told her I also talk to the pastor and told him what happened but I didn't tell my Pastor it was M.T., I told him it was someone in school. I wished that my father was there so I could run to when these people touched me but he wasn't there for me, he was in prison for abusing my mom. Yet I knew that although I felt

God wasn't listening to me, wasn't seeing what I was going through or didn't care, I really knew God was there and that HE is and will deal with the both of them, even when they both think it's over, this has to come back to them because they are valuable parts of why my life is as it is today. I was young, I was innocent, Joey knew he was wrong, rather he had a problem or not, he knew enough of the wrong he was doing and of course M.T. knew he was wrong and God will get vengeance one day for them hurting me.

I started believing that God gives his best people the hardest trials because those are the ones that will come out as pure gold in the end, even though it seems to take a very long time, but I still trust that God will allow this to be my testimony for someone else to know that they can get through this and to always just continue to trust in God, he will see you through. Yes I've contemplated suicide, yes I wanted to die, yes I'm gay because the thought of a man touching me makes me sick BUT I know God will see me through this and God is opening doors for me. I don't hate men anymore because as my mom always said, "I can't blame every man for what a couple did to me" because I love my brothers, uncles, granddaddy, my Pastors and others.

I'll stop here for now because it's brining back too many memories and it hurts. My mom said it's because I'm not healed or delivered from that hurt yet and I'm not sure if I ever will because it cuts like a knife because he didn't have to do this to me! I also have to leave the full story for my own book release that will come soon ☺

Tae book coming soon!

There's A Stranger In My House

"The Silent Screams Series"
Part III

The Silent Screams Series Part III

www.bethanysgroup.com
Yolanda@bethanysgroup.com

Author: Yolanda Lee~George

This concluded the Silent Screams Series

Part I – Someone to Love the Little Girl In Me

Part II – Someone Almost Loved me to Death

Part III – There's A Stranger in my house!

Coming soon!
The Aftermath of the Silent Screams!
The Spiritual Manifestation of the Silent Screams!
And more!!!!

www.ingramcontent.com/pod-product-compliance
Lightning Source LLC
Chambersburg PA
CBHW032207040426
42449CB00005B/473